basic

BIRD ID

in Southern Africa

Peter G...

august 2019

Peter Ginn and **Geoff McIlleron**

GW00669636

Published by Struik Nature
(an imprint of Penguin Random House SA (Pty) Ltd)
Company Reg. No. 1953/000441/07
The Estuaries No.4, Century Avenue,
Oxbow Crescent, Century City, 7441 South Africa
PO Box 1144, Cape Town, 8000 South Africa

Visit www.penguinrandomhouse.co.za and join the StruikNature
Club for updates, news, events and special offers.

First published in 2011
3 4 5 6 7 8 9 10

Publishing manager: Pippa Parker
Managing editor: Helen de Villiers
Editor: Julia Casciola
Designer: Janice Evans

Reproduction by Hirt & Carter Cape (Pty) Ltd
Printed and bound by **DJE Flexible Print Solutions,**
Pietermaritzburg, South Africa

ISBN: 978 1 77007 862 8 (PRINT)
ISBN: 978 1 43170 109 4 (ePUB)
ISBN: 978 1 43170 110 0 (ePDF)

Key to photographic credits in text: Peter J Ginn (PJG),
Nico Myburgh (NM), Will Nichol (WN), Albert Froneman/
Images of Africa (AF/IOA), Nigel Dennis/IOA (ND/IOA)

Front cover photo credits:
(top left): *Orange-breasted Sunbird in flight* (**NM***)
(centre right): *African Barred Owlet* (**PJG**)

Back cover photo credit:
(top right): *Southern White-faced Owl* (**NM**)

Images on this page:
(top to bottom): *White-fronted Plover,*
White-fronted Bee-eater, Swee Waxbill, Cape Eagle-Owl

Images on the opposite page:
(top to bottom): *Crimson-breasted Shrike,*
Great Egret, Bennett's Woodpecker

CONTENTS

ACKNOWLEDGEMENTS

I am grateful to my uncle, George Whitehouse, who first sparked my love of birding as a child on his farm, Nylsvlei, in the Limpopo region of South Africa. It was a wonderful piece of wilderness and farmland, today acknowledged to be one of South Africa's premier birding places, and I spent many happy school holidays there searching for nests and watching birds under his guidance.

Soon after starting school I was given a copy of the *Birds of Southern Africa* by Austin Roberts, which I devoured almost in one session while hospitalised after a tonsillectomy. This was the way I and many birders learned identification until well into the 1970s and 1980s, and I am thankful for the invaluable contribution it made to me. But it was incredibly tedious paging through the plates trying to find the bird I was looking for! I soon realised that I needed to be able to identify the bird's family so that I could turn to the right plate first time. Thus began the journey leading to a system of bird identification, and this book.

My thanks also go to Will Nichol, a salon photographer who took up bird photography after his retirement to Nature's Valley, where we holidayed. I helped him to identify birds, find nests and set up hides – and he introduced me to the basics of his art. The rest, as they say, is history.

Later, while teaching in Zimbabwe from 1962 to 1990, I met all sorts of birders and naturalists who helped to develop the system of bird ID presented in this book. My thanks go to them all – the boys at the school who did the 'field trials' and ironed out many of the initial problems, and the birders who have been afield with me over the last 40 years, especially Des Jackson. Although they may not recognise their individual contributions, I would like to pay tribute to the ways in which they helped me.

A pair of Purple-crested Turacos resting on a perch in woodland

PREFACE

Over the last five decades I have spent an enormous amount of time showing beginners how to get started in bird watching. This book distils that experience into a single volume, providing the beginner with a basic and relatively simple system of identification. There is no magic formula, but if you learn the basics presented here you will be able to identify most of the birds in your garden and neighbourhood, and then further afield.

Worldwide, bird watching has become a popular outdoor activity. Many birders are now doing more than just identifying birds, they are also observing bird habits and habitat, feeding and breeding behaviour, distribution, etc. At the same time the advent of digital cameras has made photographing birds relatively simple so that even beginners can take good photographs, enabling them to identify birds later at home and also providing a record of species they have seen.

Here in southern Africa birders have an outstanding range of field guides to choose from, for example, *'Newman's Birds'* and *'Sasol Birds'*, and reference books such as *'Roberts Birds'* and *The Complete Guide to Southern African Birds*. But these books do not teach the beginner how to identify birds. This volume is designed to fill the gap and enable anyone to learn basic bird identification in their home area, even if they do not have an expert birder to help them. It does not attempt to illustrate or discuss all southern African bird species, nor does it illustrate all the variation found in local birds. For reasons of simplicity and so as not to confuse the beginner, it focuses on the distinctive and more common families and makes only passing reference to difficult families like the pipits, larks, cisticolas, warblers and those in the wader group.

Southern Carmine Bee-eaters jostling for space on a branch

GETTING STARTED

Many people are eager to start watching birds, but don't know *how* to begin. The system in this book is designed to meet that need and will provide you with a methodology that, with practise, will become instinctive.

Start by observing familiar birds in your area, such as sparrows and doves, and get to know them well by their *shape, size* and *movements*. From there you can expand the list of birds you can identify, using those you already know for comparison, until most of the birds common in your area are known.

Four essential pieces of equipment

☐ **A basic system of bird identification,** such as the one presented in this book.

☐ **A field guide:** *'Newman's Birds'* is often the first choice for beginners because of its larger and simpler illustrations, although some prefer *Sasol Birds of Southern Africa* or *'Roberts Field Guide'*.

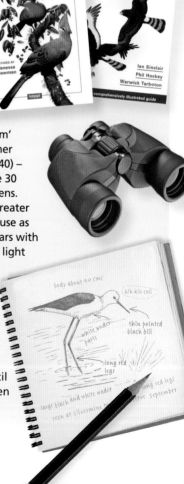

☐ **Binoculars:** An essential item, enabling you to observe birds closely without disturbing them. 'Roof-prism' binoculars with straight tubes are better than 'porro-prism' binoculars with angled tubes. The beginner is advised to invest in a pair of 8 x 30 (or 40) – the 8 being magnification power and the 30 the diameter in millimetres of the front lens. Although a 10-power pair may provide greater magnification, they are more difficult to use as they have a smaller field of view. Binoculars with small exit lenses (25 mm) allow much less light through and have a smaller field of view. They are therefore much less suitable for bird watching than 8 x 30 or 40.

☐ **A notebook:** An A6-sized notebook is invaluable in the field. Note down size and shape and anything unusual, such as a very long tail or specific behaviour. It's a good idea to make a labelled pencil sketch, which you can refer to later when consulting a field guide.

Understanding bird groups

Birds, like all living organisms, can be arranged into related groups based on shared features. It is important to understand bird groups and characteristics of different groups as it is always easier to place a bird in a particular group before recognising the individual species.

What is a family? Birds with visible and structural similarities are grouped into families. Doves and pigeons, for instance, both belong to the family Columbidae, and ducks and geese belong to Anatidae. All kingfishers belong to Halcyonidae and share common features and behave in a similar way.

What is a species? Families are divided into genera (singular 'genus'); so, several genera make up one family. Similarly, several species make up one genus. Members of one species breed only with their own species and not with others in their genus. Thus the Speckled Pigeon (*Columba guinea*) will breed with other Speckled Pigeons, but not with Feral Pigeons (*Columba livia*). Notice that each species name is made up of two parts – the first name indicates the genus (*Columba* in the example above), and the second indicates the species. Genus and species names are always written in *italics*.

What is a group? This is a loose, non-scientific term used informally to lump together a number of species and sometimes families that share a particular feature. For example, birds of prey form a 'group' of meat-eating birds, while seabirds are a broad, mixed group that share a common habitat.

Example of family group relationships (part of *Estrildidae* family)

FAMILY
Orange-breasted Waxbill
Jameson's Firefinch
Green Twinspot

Waxbills, Firefinches and Twinspots

GENUS
Amadina
Lagonistica
Granatina

SPECIES
Red-headed Finch
Cut-throat Finch
Red-billed Firefinch
African Firefinch
Violet-eared Waxbill

1 INTRODUCTION

Southern Africa's bird fauna represents approximately 10 per cent of all described bird species in the world. It includes the largest bird in the world, the Common Ostrich, and some of the smallest, the Penduline Tits (weighing only 6 g), and comprises more than 900 different species. Coming to terms with so many birds may seem daunting at first, but it is easier than you think and can be mastered using a step-by-step approach (such as this one), and careful note-taking.

The system presented here trains you how to observe birds – *what* to look for, and *how* to look at these different features in relation to each other. For instance, how to observe size, shape, posture, the bill, wings, feet, etc., forming what is commonly known as a 'field description'. This description will enable you to identify the bird's *family* in your field guide, and from there, in most cases, the species. So the book offers a vital step, without which a field guide can seem inaccessible. The colour photos support the text in this process, training you to observe and memorise features of local birds.

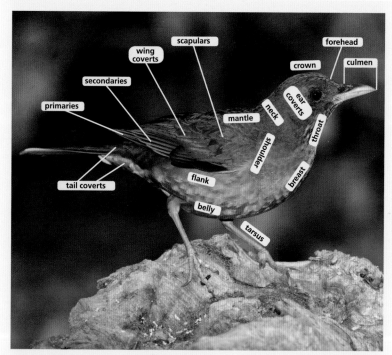

It is important to know the parts of a bird when using this system – the diagram above of an Olive Thrush gives the main features you will need to observe.

Most people tend to notice the colours of a bird first, especially where these are bright and bold – however, colour can be confusing in identifying family groups because different birds within one family may present with a variety of colours. Furthermore, many birds, particularly those with iridescent plumage, change colour as the incident light changes, and others have brightly coloured breeding finery that is seen only for a few months, after which the males moult back into their drab, non-breeding plumage.

Where colour can be useful is in isolating certain individual species, such as the striking male Narina Trogon and Crimson-breasted Shrike, which have particularly characteristic-coloured plumage.

Southern Red Bishop in brightly coloured breeding plumage (left), and later in drab, non-breeding plumage (right). This shows why using colour to identify birds can be confusing.

Birds with iridescent plumage, such as this Greater Blue-eared (Glossy) Starling, change colour depending on the light.

2 BASIC SYSTEM OF BIRD ID

The system of identification outlined below has been developed over years and used successfully by many beginners. It encourages you to focus on and note certain physical features and individual parts of a bird. This will lead to the next step, which involves identifying the family or bird group, and then to identification of the species. This process requires discipline at first but in time becomes second nature. Note that the bill is the most important single feature in defining bird families. Because of this, a whole chapter has been dedicated to bills (see page 38).

Summary of features used in bird ID

☐ **Size** Compare the bird's size with that of well-known species such as Cape White-eye, Cape Sparrow, Cape Turtle Dove, Crowned Lapwing and Helmeted Guineafowl.

☐ **Shape** Note the bird's overall shape, including head, body and tail – this may be rounded, elongated, etc.

☐ **Posture** Observe how a bird stands or sits, for example, the posture may be upright or angled.

☐ **Head** Note the size and shape and any unusual features, such as a crest.

☐ **Bill** Shape and size provide clues to the bird's diet and ways of obtaining food. Discussed in Chapter 3.

☐ **Neck** Observe the length and shape of the neck relative to the head and body – is it long, short, thick, etc.?

☐ **Body** Consider the shape of the body itself (excluding the head and tail), for instance, a noticeably rounded or elongated body.

☐ **Wings** Describe the wings, noting shape and size, for example, are they tapering or rounded, and are they patterned, etc.?

☐ **Tail** Note the shape, length and width of the tail; it may be short, long, forked, etc.

☐ **Legs and feet** Consider the length and shape of the legs, and size and positioning of the toes. These give clues to the feeding habits.

☐ **Colour** This plays an important role in identifying the actual species.

Size

Although most bird books give the bird's length (usually from the tip of the bill to the tip of the tail, in millimetres), it is difficult to estimate a bird's size in millimetres unless it is in the hand. It is much better, therefore, to learn how to relate the size of the bird you are watching to a number of species you see regularly. To assist with this, the box below illustrates five well-known local birds ranging in size from the Cape White-eye (length 125 mm) to the Helmeted Guineafowl (560 mm). Look at birds in your garden, preferably with the binoculars you will be using in the field, and get a feel for their size relative to the size of these well-known birds (or others common in your area). For instance, the beginner could decide that a bird is larger than a dove and smaller than a lapwing.

In the same way, when you are trying to assess the size of any part of the bird, it is almost impossible to estimate this in millimetres. You should relate the size to other parts of the bird, usually those closest to the part you are observing. Thus, when looking at the length of the bird's bill, you would compare it with the length of the head from the base of the bill to the back of the head. Is the bill shorter than the head, about the same length, longer, or very much longer than the head? If it is longer, is it twice, three times or four times as long as the head?

Common birds of varying sizes all produced to scale

Cape White-eye

Cape Sparrow

Cape Turtle Dove

Crowned Lapwing

Helmeted Guineafowl

Shape

This is very difficult to describe *precisely*. It is the *general* shape of the bird that matters; although most birds are similar, some appear elongated, such as egrets, others rounded or fatter, for instance, spurfowl. Familiarise yourself with the standard or basic shape and then relate other shapes to it.

White-throated Robin-Chat – standard shape

Crested Francolin has a rounded shape

Goliath Heron showing an elongated body

Gizz

You may hear birders talking about the gizz (giss or jizz) of a bird. This is a bird's **G**eneral **S**ize and **S**hape and the **way it moves**. It is the overall impression gathered at a glance – much as one identifies a person by their 'style', movement and mannerisms. Gizz is especially useful for identifying groups and families, for instance, you might recognise a bird as a hornbill by its gizz but not know which species of hornbill it is.

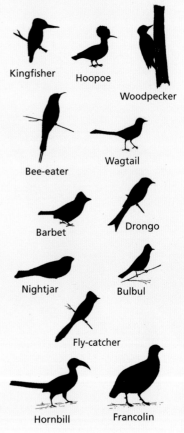

Kingfisher Hoopoe Woodpecker

Bee-eater Wagtail

Barbet Drongo

Nightjar Bulbul

Fly-catcher

Hornbill Francolin

Silhouettes by Graeme Arnott

Distinctive shapes: Some birds are distinctively shaped as a result of a feature, such as a crest at the back of the head or a distinctively shaped tail.

African Hoopoe

Fork-tailed Drongo

Shape of nocturnal birds: Birds that are active at night must be recognised by shape, size and call as there is too little light to see colour at night. Several owls have 'ear' tufts that give them a characteristic silhouette, such as the Southern White-faced Owl (below left). Contrast this with the African Barred Owlet (below right), which is of similar size, but lacks the tufts.

Southern White-faced Owl

African Barred Owlet

Posture

A bird is the sum of all its parts and merely using size and shape will not necessarily enable you to identify it. It is also important to see how the bird sits or stands (we are still dealing with a stationary bird – movement will be discussed later). This posture or stance can be very revealing and in some cases it is peculiar not only to a family, but also to an individual species.

Standard/angled posture: Most passerines or perching birds have this posture – consider the way a thrush or pipit stands with the head held high, the legs slightly bent, and the back at about 45 degrees to the ground.

Kurrichane Thrush

African Pipit

Upright posture: Birds of prey, such as eagles and owls, stand almost upright. Egrets and herons also have an upright stance.

Martial Eagle

Little Egret

Grey Heron

Horizontal posture: Doves and greenshank are good examples of birds with horizontal posture.

African Mourning Dove

Common Greenshank

Bear in mind that birds change posture as they move or start feeding – for instance, herons, spoonbills and egrets are upright when standing still, but more or less horizontal when hunting. Turacos run along branches holding their body parallel to the branch, while mousebirds hang. When on the ground some birds appear to be 'crouching', for example, sandgrouse, while others, such as the nightjars, adopt a 'squatting' posture.

Squacco Heron feeding in typical horizontal posture

Head

The shape of a bird's head is determined by a number of features, such as skull shape, feathering/crests, position of the eyes and bill type (the latter is explored fully in Chapter 3).

Always remember to note the size of the head relative to the neck, and to the size and shape of the bill. Remember also to keep the 'standard' head shape of the thrush family in mind, and to note shapes that deviate from that standard.

Crests: These can have a marked effect on head shape and can be a clue to a bird's identity. In some families, such as the eagles, a crest is more the exception than the rule, i.e. one species may be crested and the others not. However, other families are characterised by their crests and all species in that family will display one, such as turacos and mousebirds.

Knysna Turaco　　　*Livingstone's Turaco*　　　*Purple-crested Turaco*

Note that while many species, like the Crested Barbet, keep the crest up permanently, a few, like the African Hoopoe and Kori Bustard, can raise and lower it.

African Hoopoe with crest up　　　*The same species with the crest lowered*

Eye position: This affects the overall look of the head. Predatory birds, such as eagles and owls, have forward-facing eyes to provide binocular vision, enabling accurate judgement of distances, whereas species that are preyed upon, such as pipits, have eyes on the sides of the head to spot predators approaching from any direction.

Tawny Eagle   *African Barred Owlet*   *Striped Pipit*

Distinctive facial features: Unusual features such as wattles (flaps of bare skin that hang down the face, such as on the White-crowned Lapwing), or a casque (a horny protrusion on top of the head as can be seen on the Helmeted Guineafowl), can also give the head a characteristic look that is important in identification.

White-crowned Lapwing   *Helmeted Guineafowl*   *Crested Guineafowl*

Bare facial skin: Bare skin on the face can be diagnostic in some birds. For instance, the red skin on the face and throat of the Lappet-faced Vulture is diagnostic. Other birds are characterised by areas of bare skin around the beak and eye, such as in the Yellow-billed Stork and Red-faced Mousebird.

Lappet-faced Vulture   *Yellow-billed Stork*   *Red-faced Mousebird*

Bill See Chapter 3 for detailed information on bills and ID.

Neck

The neck is best described by comparing its length and thickness with the size of the head and body.

Thickness of the neck: A bird's neck usually appears to be about the same thickness/diameter as its head. Consider the three diverse examples below – the Pied Crow has a thick-set neck, the African Wattled Lapwing a relatively thick neck, and the Great Egret a thin neck. Notice how in each case the neck and head are of roughly similar diameter.

Pied Crow   African Wattled Lapwing   Great Egret

Neck posture: Note how the neck is held, particularly when flying. For example, storks and cormorants fly with the neck held straight, while herons, egrets and darters fly with the neck in an S-shape.

Abdim's Stork in flight, with the neck   Purple Heron in flight, showing an
held straight   S-shaped neck

Length of the neck: Consider whether the neck is shorter than the head length (nightjars); the same length as the head (robins and thrushes); longer than the head (geese); or very much longer than the head (herons). The length of a bird's neck is closely related to its feeding habits.

Normal/standard length neck: Most passerines, such as thrushes, flycatchers, robins, orioles and brownbuls, have a standard length neck.

Marico Flycatcher

Terrestrial Brownbul

African Golden Oriole

Long neck: The neck appears longer than the head in birds such as geese, pelicans, francolin and guineafowl, oystercatchers, some waders, plovers, gulls and skuas.

Great White Pelican

Egyptian Goose

Whimbrel

Very long neck: The neck is very much longer than the head in ostriches, cranes, storks and bustards, flamingos, korhaans, darters, herons and egrets.

Common Ostrich

Grey Crowned Crane

Wattled Crane

Black-bellied Bustard

Greater Flamingo

While darters closely resemble cormorants in the water, the darter's neck is very much longer and thinner than that of the cormorant, and it has a spear-shaped bill, while the cormorant has a hooked-tip bill.

African Darter

White-breasted Cormorant

Short neck: In some species the neck at rest appears to be slightly shorter than the head – but be aware that birds can crane or stretch the neck! Typical examples of short-necked birds are flycatchers, kingfishers, bee-eaters, woodpeckers, penguins, mousebirds, sandgrouse, petrels and terns, doves and birds of prey.

Marico Flycatcher

Pied Kingfisher

White-fronted Bee-eater

Bennett's Woodpecker

African Penguin

Speckled Mousebird

Very short neck: In the following birds the neck is apparently shorter than the head – indeed, there often appears to be no neck: parrots, swallows, owls, quails and buttonquails, nightjars and swifts.

Brown-headed Parrot

Lesser Striped Swallow

Barn Owl

Black-rumped Buttonquail

Body

You will probably find that describing body shape in detail is not easy in the field. However, if you relate the body shape of the bird you are observing to the shape of a species you know well, you will be able to pick up any differences. Body size is best related to the length of the head, neck and tail. Note whether the body appears to be elongated (egrets); a standard shape (many starlings); or rounded (spurfowl/francolin and quails).

Standard body shape: Most passerines have this structure.

Southern Boubou

White-starred Robin

Elongated body shape: Egrets, herons and many birds of prey have an elongated body shape.

Great Egret fishing with its neck extended ahead of the elongated body so that it can see potential prey before the legs disturb the fish or frog.

Rounded body shape: Guineafowl, francolin, quails, sandgrouse, pittas, some doves, and many of the weaver, waxbill and finch groups have a characteristically rounded body shape.

Helmeted Guineafowl

African Pitta

Swee Waxbill

Note that most birds can alter their body shape by fluffing up their feathers; and some birds can alter their shape significantly in this way!

Yellow-crowned Bishop with feathers flat

The same bird with its feathers puffed up

Wings

Although the *structure* of practically all bird wings is similar, there is huge variation in the *shape*. Try to note whether the wings appear long or short relative to body size. Francolin, for example, have relatively short wings while kites have long wings. Next, try to estimate wing width relative to length, that is, do the wings appear to be wide/broad compared with the length, such as in the Hadeda Ibis; or narrow compared with length, such as in falcons; or very narrow, as in swifts?

Elongated and tapering wings: This wing shape is evident to varying degrees on swifts, falcons, swallows, frigate birds, skimmers and some cuckoos. It is particularly pronounced in swifts, which are superb fliers. Notice how migratory birds, especially passerines, often have more pointed wings than their resident relatives.

Alpine Swift

African Skimmer

Long wings: Soaring birds, like vultures, kites, some eagles, storks and albatrosses, have long wings.

Verreaux's Eagle

White-backed Vulture

Broad wings with rounded tips: This wing shape is found on birds of prey that hunt in forest and woodland, as well as on herons, francolin and guineafowl.

Notice how broad the Crowned Eagle's wings are relative to their length. Short wings enable the bird to manouvre between trees.

Unusual features on the wings: Notice any unusual features, like pinion (finger) feathers at the ends of wings, as well as distinctive wing shapes, like those of the Bateleur and Verreux's eagles.

Secretarybird in a stand-off with a black-backed jackal. Notice the long, straight wings with pinions at the ends.

Patterns on the wings: Observe whether the wings have distinctive patterns in either black and white or colour. These can be important in identification.

Spotted Eagle-Owl

Pintado Petrel

Black-chested Snake Eagle

Northern Black Korhaan

Wings in flight: It is difficult to determine wing shape when a bird is in flight – other than in the soaring and gliding birds where the wings are periodically extended motionless and are therefore easier to see.

Southern Carmine Bee-eater gliding

Shy Albatross gliding on its huge wingspan

Also bear in mind that birds change their wing shape to manoeuvre as they fly, that is, they 'open' or 'close' their feathers. The wings are pulled closer to the body as they dive, and very close to the body when 'stooping' onto prey. When coming in to land birds pull their wings slightly backwards and fan the tail to increase 'drag' and slow down.

Osprey with its wings wide open but held slightly backwards, enabling the bird to glide down to a perch to eat the fish gripped in its talons.

Wing action: Notice the rate of wing beats – is it rapid (sunbirds and small kingfishers), or slow (egrets)? Some birds alternate flapping their wings and then gliding, such as the hornbills, while birds such as ducks and francolin with relatively heavy bodies and small wings flap their wings continuously.

African Pygmy Kingfisher using its wings to 'brake' as the bird enters the nest burrow. The wing action changes from very rapid when in flight, to very slow at this point.

Tail

The most noticeable proportion of the tail is its length, although some tails are much broader than others. Try to relate the length of the tail to the body length – is the tail about the same length as the body (a standard tail), is it longer or much longer, or is it shorter or much shorter than the body? Notice how the legs and feet of long-legged birds like cranes and herons extend well beyond the tail in flight. In addition to tail length, also notice the width (the Broad-tailed Warbler, for instance, has a relatively broad tail), and look for colour patterns.

Standard tail: The tail is about the same length as the body in most passerines.

Mocking Cliff Chat   *Cape Robin-Chat*

Long tail: The tail is noticeably longer than the body in some rollers, bee-eaters and sunbirds, as well as in turacos, trogons, wood-hoopoes, some waxbills and the Namaqua Dove (the only local dove with a long tail).

Lilac-breasted Roller   *Male Narina Trogon*   *Green Wood-hoopoe (juv.)*

Very long tail: The tail is at least twice as long as the body in the African Paradise Flycatcher, the male Cape Sugarbird, breeding male whydahs, mousebirds and some male widowbirds in breeding plumage.

Male African Paradise Flycatcher   *Male Cape Sugarbird*   *Male Pin-tailed Whydah*

Short to very short tail: The tail is noticeably shorter than the body or very much shorter in the case of some warblers (including the crombec), vultures, many eagles, owls, grebes, batis, ducks, quails, francolin, white-eyes and quail-finches.

Long-billed Crombec

Bateleur

Black-rumped Buttonquail

Long, thin 'pin' feathers in the tail: Some long-tailed birds, such as sunbirds, bee-eaters, rollers, male whydahs in breeding plumage and most swallows, have long, thin 'pin' feathers in the tail.

Male Malachite Sunbird

Lesser Striped Swallow

European Bee-eater

Distinctively shaped tail: Most tails are straight and rounded at the end, but some birds have distinctively shaped tails, for instance, woodpeckers with their sharp, spiky tail feathers, some male whydahs in breeding plumage, and some rollers, bee-eaters and drongos. The tails of certain species (among them rollers and bee-eaters) are so characteristic as to be diagnostic.

Swallow-tailed Bee-eater

Male breeding Shaft-tailed Whydah

Fork-tailed Drongo

Movement of the tail: Some birds move their tails in a characteristic way, such as wagtails, which wag the tail up and down as they walk; and pipits, which stand still before wagging the tail. Some robins flick the tail before take-off.

Chorister Robin-Chat flicking its tail just before taking off

Tail 'angles': Some birds cock the tail or move it around as a signal to their mate or others of the same species.

Crested Francolin cocking its tail

White-browed Scrub Robin uses the tail to signal mates. The tail may be cocked, as shown, or lowered below the horizontal. When excited the tail may be raised or lowered rapidly or moved from side to side. When danger threatens, the bird fans the tail and droops the wings to expose white feathers as a sign of danger.

Karoo Prinia cocks and 'wags' the tail

Legs and feet

The length and shape of the legs often provide a guide to how the bird feeds. Birds that wade after fish normally have long legs, for example, herons and flamingos, while those that pick seed off the ground have short legs, such as doves and waxbills. It is also important to notice the position of the legs on the body.

Standard leg length: These legs are shorter above the knee than below and are a bit shorter than the length of the body, as in chats, thrushes and robins.

African Stonechat

Cape Rock Thrush

White-starred Robin

Long legs, much longer than the body: Birds like stilt and avocet, flamingos, egrets, some herons, some waders, coursers, lapwings, storks and Secretarybirds have legs that are much longer than the body.

Black-winged Stilt

Greater Flamingo

Short legs: Many birds have short legs, including kingfishers, sunbirds, sandgrouse, terns, cuckoos, coucals, doves, parrots and waxbills.

Grey-headed Kingfisher

Collared Sunbird

Namaqua Sandgrouse

Very short legs: Swallows, nightjars, owls, swifts, oxpeckers, woodpeckers and creepers have particularly short legs. Swifts have such short, weak legs that they cannot perch and seldom alight, even sleeping during flight.

Red-breasted Swallow

Swamp Nightjar

Pearl-spotted Owlet

Leg position: Notice how the legs of penguins and grebes are placed far back on the body.

African Penguin

Great Crested Grebe with foot extended

Feet: Most birds have three toes facing forward and one back. The exceptions are the ostrich (two forward); woodpeckers and barbets (two forward and two back); and buttonquail (three forward).

Bennett's Woodpecker

Buff-spotted Flufftail

33

Taloned feet: All birds have clawed toes for scratching in the soil for food, but the strong, highly specialised claws (talons) on birds of prey are designed to grasp and kill. Other than in vultures (which don't actually kill prey), the talons are extremely sharp for piercing victims. Birds of prey don't use the beak when hunting – large eagles, like the Crowned Eagle, have feet strong enough to crush the neck or back of a small bushbuck. Kestrels use their feet to catch flying-ants on the wing, and then bend down to eat their prey while still flying.

Verreaux's Eagle   *Lanner Falcon*

Webbed feet: Ducks, geese, darters, cormorants, gannets, gulls, albatrosses and flamingos have webs between their toes, which enable them to swim well. These birds also use their webbed feet to lift off, either by pushing against the water with both feet – cormorants and darters do this conspicuoulsy – or by running across the water until they have enough speed to get airborne, like flamingos. These webs also prevent them from sinking into the mud when wading.

Fulvous Whistling Duck   *African Darter*

Lobed feet: Grebes, coots and finfoot have partial webs called lobes – three pairs on each toe. The lobes expand as the feet push backwards through the water.

All coots have long lobed toes enabling them to swim well but also walk well on land.

Long-toed feet: African and Lesser jacanas, some crakes and flufftails, and Long-toed Lapwings have particularly long toes. The African Jacana, for example, walks on floating water plants, with the bird's long toes distributing its weight across a large area so that it does not sink.

African Jacana

Black Crake

Striated Heron

Colour

Remember that colour is more useful for identifying species than families. As always, start with birds you know, and familiarise yourself with their colours first.

Greater Double-collared Sunbird

Southern Carmine Bee-eaters

Observe the colours of the head, neck, breast, wings and tail as in most species it is these parts that bear the diagnostic patterns. It is valuable to make notes or sketches in the field that you can refer to later.

Initially you do not need to use a huge range of colours. Begin with the basic ones – black, white, brown, rufous, red, orange, yellow, navy blue, blue and green. Whatever names you give colours, try to be consistent in using them so that you can refer back to them later for identifying a bird you could not identify in the field. Observe whether the plumage is iridescent, and note the colour of bare parts such as the bill and feet. Later, as you become more experienced, you may well find it quicker to note the colours of each part of the bird as you describe size and shape.

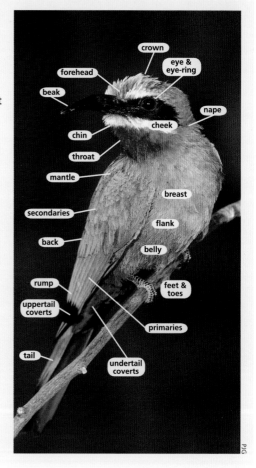

The colours of a bird's feathers are formed in two ways – either from pigments, or from light reflected by the keratin (translucent protein of which feathers are made). Bright yellow, orange and red feathers are produced by carotenoid pigments in the bird's diet. Flamingos are a striking example of this.

Lesser Flamingos feeding at Kamfer's Dam near Kimberley where they breed.

Flight feathers in many birds are black, as the dark pigment, melanin, gives them extra strength. The tips of the flight feathers have to be particularly strong as they bear the brunt of the flight action. African Sacred Ibis, for instance, have strong black tips to their flight feathers as they commute from a central roost, flying as much as 120 km daily to reach feeding areas. White feathers don't contain any pigment and wear down more easily.

Notice the melanin-pigmented tips to the flight feathers of these African Sacred Ibis.

3 BILLS AND BIRD ID

In many cases the shape of a bird's bill can be used to determine the family to which the bird belongs – indeed in some cases the bill is so distinctive that the species can be determined too, for example, the spoonbill. However, it is useful to start by referring to a basic or standard bill shape, and the thrushes and bulbuls common in our gardens provide just such a shape. All other bill groups are described as being in some way different from this 'basic model'.

Summary of bill groups

- **Basic bill** Simple, straight bill with upper mandible slightly arched.

- **Forceps or pointed bill** Short, straight bill with sharp point.

- **Bill with hooked upper mandible** Strong bill with the upper mandible curved along its entire length.

- **Hooked-tip bill** The tip of the upper mandible curves down over the lower one.

- **Bill with arched upper mandible** Highly arched upper mandible to provide extra strength for digging.

- **Spear or dagger-shaped bill** Straight, sharply pointed bill, often long.

- **Small, sharply pointed bill** Found on insectivorous birds, used to probe holes in bark, etc.

- **Probing bill – thin and usually straight** A thin bill used to probe soft earth or mud in search of food.

- **Curved bill: curved downwards (decurved); curved upwards (recurved)** Usually thin to probe flowers (sunbirds), but thicker in birds that probe soil or mud (ibises).

- **Conical/pyramidal bill** Short, strong bill for cracking husks off grain.

- **Flattened bill** Typically a duck's bill, with or without a hooked tip.

- **Flattened bill with large gape** A small, short bill; opens to reveal gape.

- **Specialist bill** A range of specially adapted bills, in various shapes.

Bill shape is the most varied single visible feature on birds because it is adapted to the diet of the species and to the often unique ways in which they obtain food. For instance, the slender, curved bill of the sunbird enables it to probe deeply into flowers to access nectar, while the dagger-like bill of the Caspian Tern is adapted for diving into water to catch fish.

Collared Sunbird

Caspian Tern

The bill consists of two parts – an upper and a lower mandible. These are usually the same length, but in a few cases, such as the African Skimmer, they are of different length. The lower mandible is usually more or less straight unless the whole bill is curved. The upper mandible varies a lot and may be straight, the same thickness or thicker than the lower mandible, arched upwards for strength, hooked, or hooked only at the tip, etc. The bill may be straight, decurved (curved downwards) or recurved (curved upwards). It is this variety of shapes that enables birds to exploit many environmental niches for feeding and that helps birdwatchers to identify many families on the strength of a single feature.

An African Skimmer settling into its nest – notice its long, lower mandible

The use of different descriptive terms to identify 'bill groups' has engendered much discussion over the years. The terms used in this book are ones that have generally found favour with beginners being taught to identify birds. However, do not be put off by names – the bill shape is what is important!

Basic bill

The 'basic' or standard bill of the bulbul is found in most passerines (perching birds or songbirds) and is likely to be encountered in many garden species. The bill is fairly thin and seldom conspicuous. The upper mandible is straight and may be slightly arched to make it stronger. Sometimes it is slightly hooked at the tip. The lower mandible is straight. The bill's shape points to an omnivorous diet – these birds pick up a variety of food, from fruit to insects and small reptiles.

Common examples are the thrushes, robins, bulbuls, babblers, many warblers, cisticolas and prinias, wagtails, starlings, wheatears, chats, some flycatchers and larks, pipits and longclaws.

Kurrichane Thrush

Striped Pipit

Cape Robin-Chat

African Red-eyed Bulbul

Arrow-marked Babbler

Black-chested Prinia

African Pied Wagtail

Greater Blue-eared Starling

Capped Wheatear

Forceps or pointed bill

These bills are similar to the basic shape, but the upper mandible is usually straight so the bill appears longer and straighter than usual. Many of these birds pick up minute insects, crustaceans and other small prey, often in or along the water's edge. This group also includes some families that feed on seeds and small fruit on the ground; they cannot crack the outer husk of the seed so have to soften the husk in their crop before swallowing the kernel.

Examples here are the grebes (note that the bill of the Great-crested Grebe is longer and more dagger-like than that of other grebes), crakes and allies (related birds), buttonquails, bustards and korhaans, lapwings, plovers and some waders, jacanas, thick-knees, coursers, some weavers such as the Spectacled Weaver, and doves and sandgrouse (which are essentially seed-eaters, but some doves also eat insects and fruit).

Little Grebe

Black Crake

Kurrichane Buttonquail

Black-bellied Bustard

Crowned Lapwing

African Jacana

Water Thick-knee

Chestnut-banded Plover

African Mourning Dove

Bill with hooked upper mandible

In some birds the whole upper mandible is curved over the lower mandible to create a strong hook used for tearing food. This includes mammalian, reptilian and avian (bird) prey in the case of most birds of prey; fish in the case of African Fish Eagle, Osprey and Pel's Fishing Owl; and fruit in the case of parrots.

You will see this bill type on eagles and Secretarybirds, kites and buzzards, goshawks and sparrowhawks, harriers, harrier-hawks and osprey, as well as vultures and parrots. Some parrot species use the beak as a 'foot' when scrambling around high branches in search of fruit and nuts. Falcons also have a hooked upper mandible, but with a distinctive notch behind the hook to sever the neck vertebrae of prey.

Verreaux's Eagle

African Hawk-Eagle

Secretarybird

Tawny Eagle

Black-shouldered Kite

Pale Chanting Goshawk

Little Sparrowhawk

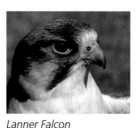

Lanner Falcon

Cape Vulture

Lappet-faced Vulture

Pearl-spotted Owlet

Brown-headed Parrot

Hooked-tip bill

Three groups of birds have a beak with a hooked tip that is helpful in holding prey like fish and insects, or tearing fruit open. The degree to which the tip is hooked is very variable – some, like the Fiscal Shrike, have a very marked hooked tip, while others, like orioles, have the tip of the upper mandible gently curved over the lower mandible.

Fish-eating birds with a hooked-tip bill include the Hamerkop, albatrosses, cormorants, the African Penguin, shearwaters, petrels, gulls, skuas and frigatebirds.

Hamerkop   *Black-browed Albatross*   *White-breasted Cormorant*

Fruit-eating birds with a hooked tip to the bill are the Green Pigeon, mousebirds and turacos.

African Green Pigeon   *Speckled Mousebird*   *Schalow's Turaco*

Insect-eating birds such as boubous, drongos, shrikes, cuckoo shrikes, rollers and orioles, use the hooked tip to seize insects.

Southern Boubou   *Fork-tailed Drongo*   *Grey-headed Bushshrike*

Note: Many ducks and geese have a small hook at the tip of a flattened bill.

Bill with arched upper mandible

The arched upper mandible of this group of birds provides greater strength to the bill, which can then be used for digging in the soil for bulbs and insects. This is particularly so in some species of francolin where the upper mandible is noticeably longer than the lower one, creating a hoe-like bill.

Families that exemplify this are swamphen, spurfowl/francolin, quail, guineafowl, some coucals (others have a hooked tip, such as the Black Coucal), cuckoos (the bill can be slightly hooked at the tip), and ravens, which have a very 'deep' bill from top to bottom.

African Swamphen

Swainson's Spurfowl

Cape Spurfowl

Senegal Coucal

Grey-winged Francolin

Red-billed Spurfowl

White-necked Raven

Crested Francolin

Spear or dagger-shaped bill

A number of families have a long, straight bill resembling a spearhead or dagger. However, it is interesting that few species actually spear their prey! These birds are usually water feeders and catch fish, frogs and similar prey.

Herons, egrets and darters have long necks that can be used to shoot the bill forward to capture prey swimming in the water, while gannets, tropicbirds and terns dive down into the water from flight. Kingfishers dive from a perch or while hovering for fish and frogs, and dry-land kingfishers pounce on prey from a perch. Several storks have spear-like bills although there is some variation; similarly with cranes (also note their different head shapes). African Finfoot swim along picking insects off plants near water level. Woodpeckers are an interesting example – the bill is flattened laterally and is chisel-shaped for digging into dead wood. Crows generally have a spear-shaped bill but there is some variation among these omnivorous birds.

Grey Heron

Cape Gannet

African Darter

White Stork

Saddle-billed Stork

Black Stork

Cape Crow

Grey Crowned Crane

Wattled Crane

Blue Crane

Malachite Kingfisher

Brown-hooded Kingfisher

Cardinal Woodpecker

Small, sharply pointed bill

These birds have bills that are small (usually short and thin) relative to the head size. In many of them, for example penduline tits and white-eyes, the bill has a very sharp point to pick up small insects and penetrate soft fruit. Other birds with this bill type are the small honeyguides, wrynecks and some warblers and cisticolas.

Grey Penduline Tit

Lesser Swamp Warbler

Desert Cisticola

Zitting Cisticola

Roberts's Warbler

Green-capped Eremomela

Cape White-eye perched next to an erythrina flower

Probing bill – thin and usually straight

The waders or shorebirds specialise in picking up arthropod prey on muddy surfaces and probing in soft sand or mud for food. Most of them have comparatively thin, straight bills that penetrate the mud easily. Some have decurved bills (curved downward) and a few have recurved bills (curved upward). Waders show a large range in bill length, from the Little Stint to the Eurasian Curlew – in the field bill length is best related to the length of the head.

Examples of some waders showing relative bill length – the bill is shorter than the head in the Little Stint; a bit longer than the head in the Wood Sandpiper; 1.5–2 times the length of the head in the Common Greenshank and the Curlew Sandpiper; and 3–4 times the head length in the Black-tailed Godwit and the Eurasian Curlew.

Little Stint

Wood Sandpiper

Common Greenshank

Curlew Sandpiper

Black-tailed Godwit

Eurasian Curlew

Curved bills

Curved downwards (decurved): These birds usually have fairly long to very long bills. Most, with the exception of the bee-eaters, are designed to probe into places where food can be found. The ibis family, African Hoopoe, waders and snipe probe in soft soil or mud; sunbirds and sugarbirds probe flowers; and Spotted Creeper, Common Scimitarbill and wood-hoopoes probe into cracks in tree bark. The bee-eaters are experts at catching flying insects by ambushing them from behind and below – catching a bee by the stinging end!

African Sacred Ibis

White-fronted Bee-eater

Whimbrel

Green Wood-hoopoe

Greater Double-collared Sunbird

Collared Sunbird

Cape Sugarbird

African Hoopoe

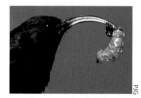

Common Scimitarbill

Curved upwards (recurved): A number of waders have slightly up-curved bills. The Pied Avocet, for example, uses the upcurved part of its bill to scythe just below the water surface for arthropod prey.

Pied Avocet

Conical/pyramidal bill

Birds with a conical bill are usually seed-eaters. These birds need a strong bill to crack the outer shell or husk of grass seeds in order to reach the nutritious kernel inside (although some, like the barbets and sparrowlarks, are omnivores).

Good examples of birds with a conical bill are the larger honeyguides, sparrowlarks and Large-billed Lark, sparrows, seed-eating species of weavers (the insectivorous species have thinner and sharper bills), bishops and widowbirds, waxbills, whydahs, finches, canaries and seed-eaters, and buntings.

Black-collared Barbet

Blue Waxbill

Cape Sparrrow

Thick-billed Weaver

Southern Red Bishop

Violet-eared Waxbill

Swee Waxbill

Shaft-tailed Whydah

Red-headed Finch

Drimstone Canary

Golden-breasted Bunting

Bronze Mannikin

Flattened bill

Although ducks are always described as having flattened bills, there is some variation in this aspect. Species that have developed goose-like feeding habits actually have an arched upper mandible to make the bill stronger for grazing grasses. Many ducks have a small hook at the tip of the upper mandible to enable the birds to grasp wet vegetation and pull seed pods off plants like water lilies.

Cape Teal

Cape Shoveler

Yellow-billed Duck

Egyptian Goose

Male Knob-billed Duck

Fulvous Whistling Duck

Female South African Shelduck nibbling grain at a feeding station

Flattened bill with large gape

These birds feed while flying, snapping up insects. The beak is usually flattened and very short. Swifts and swallows catch very small insects, often described as aerial plankton, in this way. Other examples of birds with this type of bill are nightjars, pratincoles, the African Broadbill, some flycatchers, batis and warblers.

Rufous-cheeked Nightjar

White-throated Swallow

Cape Batis

African Paradise Flycatchers

Dark-capped Yellow Warbler

White-throated Swallow chicks showing their very wide gape (angle between the upper and lower mandibles)

Specialist bill

This group consists of a number of species with individually recognisable bills that show remarkable adaptation to particular feeding methods.

Pelicans, for instance, use the soft skin pouch under the bill to scoop up fish. Great White Pelicans feed this way in flocks, while Pink-backed Pelicans are usually solitary feeders. Flamingos feed with the head upside down, using their tongue to pump water through their submerged bill, and filter out food particles. Skimmers, in turn, feed on the wing by dipping their long lower mandible into the water.

Great White Pelican

African Skimmer

Greater Flamingo feeding

Some storks feed by 'feeling' in bill-deep water with their bill slightly open, then snap it shut when they feel prey. Spoonbills also feed by feel, and avocets feed by scything the water with the bill almost submerged. Stilts have a very long, thin bill (rather like that of the probing birds), with a hooked tip to grasp arthropod prey on the surface of the water. Oystercatchers use their flattened bill to open mussels on rocks, and the Crab Plover has a very thick, dagger-shaped bill for feeding on crabs. Oxpeckers use their specially shaped bill to pick ticks and larvae off large mammals, and the omnivorous ostrich has a flattened bill to pick food up from the ground.

African Openbill

Yellow-billed Stork

Saddle-billed Stork

African Spoonbill

Pied Avocet

Black-winged Stilt

African Black Oystercatcher

Red-billed Oxpecker

Common Ostrich

Hornbills all have relatively long, large decurved bills that do not seem to be designed for special feeding methods or a particular type of food. However, the bill is very conspicuous and makes the family easy to identify, even at a distance.

A magnificent Southern Ground Hornbill with a frog and a grasshopper pincered together in its powerful bill.

4 ADDITIONAL ID POINTERS

The previous two chapters itemised and described the various physical features of the bird, providing a systematic description to work with. However, a number of useful additional factors should be considered, such as movement, feeding, calls and habitat, as these all assist in identification.

Summary of additional ID pointers

- **Movement** The particular manner in which a bird moves and the speed with which it does so can provide useful information in identification.

- **Special feeding methods** Each bird family occupies a niche in the food chain based on what it eats and how it obtains the food. In some cases, such as with pelicans, the adaptation is highly specialised.

- **Sexual dimorphism** Many birds show plumage differences between the adult male and female, with the male often being more colourful and eye-catching than the female. There can also be sexual dimorphism in shape or size.

- **Bird calls** Birds call and/or sing to proclaim territory or communicate with one another. These sounds are a valuable aid in field identification, especially in the case of more reclusive species.

- **Habitat** The type of environment in which a bird lives and to which it is suited involves adaptation to vegetation, climate, food supply and local predators.

Verreaux's Eagle arriving at its nest on a cliff, the typical habitat for this species.

Movement

(also see comments under 'Wings' in Chapter 2)

Birds move in a variety of ways: on the ground, in trees, in the air and on water. Some movements are distinctive, for instance, moorhen swim with the head moving forward and back, Common Starlings have a strutting walk, and wagtails walk with the tail wagging up and down. Some birds have distinctive display flights such as the Long-tailed Widowbird which flies slowly just above the grass with the long, heavy tail bent downnands, while others have distinctive ways of hunting, such as the Pied Kingfisher, which hovers over open water before diving in.

Long-tailed Widowbird in display flight

Pied Kingfisher hovering

Walking: Secretarybirds walk purposefully, while cranes and bustards have a stately gait, and doves and sandgrouse with short legs have a distinctive 'waddling' action. Plovers, lapwings and waders have a sort of 'stop-start' action with the body held horizontally. Penguins and grebes have their legs set relatively far back on the body and so walk upright with an ungainly gait. Many storks and waterbirds walk slowly through the water searching for prey, but some, such as the Little Egret, may walk very fast or even run in spurts.

Kori Bustard walking in open country

Black Stork hunting slowly in water

Running on the ground: Francolin, quail and guineafowl are very fast runners. Larks run rapidly and then stop to look around. Some hornbills, such as the Yellow-billed Hornbill, run across the ground with the tail cocked in the air. The Common Ostrich is the fastest land bird, reaching sprint speeds of 65 kph. It cannot fly as its smooth breastbone doesn't have a 'keel', which supports flight muscles.

Common Ostrich picking up speed

White-fronted Plover running on sand

Running in trees: Turacos are well known for their habit of running along branches and then jumping across to the next branch with the wings partially or fully spread.

Knysna Turaco about to jump from one branch to another

Hopping: Some smaller birds, such as the Cape Bunting, hop around, whereas other similar-sized birds, like the sparrows, walk.

Cape Bunting

Great Sparrow

Scrambling: Wood-hoopoes, Spotted Creepers and woodpeckers move up tree trunks with a distinctly jerky action.

Green Wood-hoopoes

Spotted Creeper

Bearded Woodpecker

Flying: While birds, such as some eagles, soar on open wings on thermals, others fly with wings flapping all the time, like ducks. Certain birds flap the wings and then 'glide' with the wings open (swallows), or with the wings shut (hornbills and woodpeckers). Initially try to describe the flight pattern in simple terms.

Black-chested Snake Eagle soaring on open wings

57

Special feeding methods
(also see comments under 'Specialist bill' in Chapter 3)

Some examples of special feeders are the African Skimmer, which catches fish by dipping its long lower mandible into the water as it flies; woodpeckers, which peck holes in wood and extract insect grubs using their very long tongue with a hook at the end; flamingos, which pump water through the beak and sieve out small items as they drag their bills upside down over the mud; pelicans, which feed in groups, working in unison to scoop fish out of the water in their pouches under the lower mandible; and nightjars, which sit on the ground so that they can see insects against the sky and then fly up to catch them. Other interesting examples are Bearded Vultures, which drop bones onto rocks from high up to break them open and get to the marrow inside, and fishing owls, which have spiny soles to enable them to grasp fish securely.

Great White Pelicans herding fish into their midst to be scooped up

Lesser Flamingos feeding in a single line to ensure that all the birds can fish in unmuddied water

Sexual dimorphism

Many species exhibit sexual dimorphism (male-female difference) in their colours, but the birds are generally the same shape and size, for example, Namaqua Dove, Narina Trogon, the sandgrouse, the small green cuckoos, woodpeckers, batis family, some flycatchers, most sunbirds, breeding widowbirds, bishops, whydahs, Violet-backed Starlings, and Black-headed and Yellow canaries. Usually the male is more brightly coloured than the female, but in some species the female initiates courtship and so is more brightly coloured, for example, the Greater Painted Snipe and Black-rumped Buttonquail.

Female Violet-backed Starling

Male Violet-backed Starling

Some birds show sexual dimorphism in their shape or size, e.g. in many eagles and other birds of prey the female is larger. The female African Jacana is also larger than the male and defends the territory. In the case of some hornbills the male has a significantly larger bill than the female (and it may be differently coloured, as in the male and female African Grey Hornbills). Tail lengths can vary between pairs in some species, for instance, the male African Paradise Flycatcher has a much longer tail than the female.

African Grey Hornbill male (top) and female (below)

The male African Paradise Flycatcher showing his long tail compared with that of the female

Bird calls

There is a huge variety of calls. Several sets of recordings are available, such as Guy Gibbon's *Southern African Bird Sounds* on cassette and CD, Gibbon's *Roberts' Multimedia Birds of Southern Africa* flash card for use on pocket computers, and *Bird Calls for Beginners* and *More Bird Calls for Beginners* (books and CDs), both by Doug Newman. Learn your local bird calls first, especially those in your garden.

Calls are extremely important in identifying birds – indeed, in the case of some 'LBJs' (Little Brown Jobs), unless the calls are heard identification is almost impossible. The night birds all have distinctive calls, providing instant identification of birds that often cannot be seen. Call is also useful in distinguishing between the three doves with a ring on the neck, namely the Cape, Red-eyed and Mourning doves, each with a very different and distinctive call.

Birds use calls for a variety of reasons – probably the most important is to define their territory, but the calls are also used to communicate with one another. A foraging group of tits or wood-hoopoes, for example, have soft contact calls so that members know where the rest of the flock is. Pairs of Tropical Boubous will duet at any time so as to remain in contact, while passerines 'sing' rather than call, a distinction that is not always clear.

Essentially, songs are more musical and complex than calls, and are usually produced by males. The female uses the song to assess the male's health and maturity. Calls, on the other hand, are usually only a few short notes to communicate information such as warning, identification, aggression, a food source, etc. A good field guide will distinguish between songs and calls.

Some birds are accurate mimics of other birds' calls, the best being the Red-capped and Chorister Robin-Chats, and the Mocking Chat which gets its name from its ability to mimic. Forked-tail Drongos and Fiscal Shrikes are also good mimics, incorporating other bird calls into their own song.

The Olive Bushshrike is found throughout the forests of southern Africa and has a remarkable variety of calls.

Habitat

Most bird species are usually found in one or more specific habitats. A simple example is that of ducks being found near water. The particular birds in each habitat are learned by experience, but some people prepare habitat lists for their home area. It is useful to have some idea as to which species you will encounter when birding in a particular region.

Listed below are the major birding habitats in southern Africa, with some of the birds you are most likely to see in each area.

Forest: Temperate (Knysna), sub-tropical Limpopo and Mpumalanga forests, Zimbabwe highlands and adjacent Mozambique. Typical birds here are the Knysna Turaco in the south, Livingstone's Turaco in the east and north, and the Yellow-throated Woodland Warbler throughout the forest regions.

Knysna Turaco

Livingstone's Turaco

Yellow-throated Woodland Warbler

Woodland: Acacia/bushveld, mopani, brachystegia/miombo. Here you will see the Acacia Pied Barbet, the Yellow-billed Hornbill, and the Miombo Tit.

Acacia Pied Barbet

Miombo Tit

Bushveld: Eastern Cape thicket, and coastal bush. The Red-throated Wryneck is at home in the Eastern Cape thicket and the Sombre Greenbul in the coastal bush.

Red-throated Wryneck   *Sombre Greenbul*

Fynbos: Protea and other fynbos groups, such as ericas. Well-known inhabitants here are the Orange-breasted Sunbird and the Cape Sugarbird.

Orange-breasted Sunbird   *Cape Sugarbird*

Highveld grassland: Short grasslands on the Highveld are the home of the Cape Longclaw and the Southern Bald Ibis.

The Cape Longclaw uses its exceptionally long claws to spread its weight so that it walks on top of the grass rather than through it.

Montane: Cape mountain fynbos, Lesotho highlands and Drakensberg, Zimbabwe and Mozambique Eastern Highlands. The Cape Rockjumper is resident in the Cape mountain fynbos, while the Bearded Vulture frequents the Drakensberg mountains and Lesotho highlands.

Cape Rockjumper

Bearded Vulture

Scrub: The Great Karoo and succulent Karoo are the natural habitat of the Karoo Chat, the Karoo Scrub Robin and the Rufous-eared Warbler.

Karoo Chat

Karoo Scrub Robin

Desert and semi-desert (Kalahari): The Namib Desert is home to Monteiro's Hornbill, and the Kalahari to the Kalahari Scrub Robin.

Monteiro's Hornbill

Kalahari Scrub Robin

Fresh water: Rivers, man-made dams and lakes, and the Wilderness lakes are home to all the waterbirds illustrated in this book, while in the Okavango Delta, Zambezi Valley and coastal Mozambique you will see the African Skimmer.

A pair of African Skimmers at the water's edge

Coastal: Sandy beaches and vegetation-covered dunes, and rocky areas. White-fronted Plovers typically frequent southern African beaches and dunes, with African Black Oystercatchers inhabiting the rocky areas.

White-fronted Plover

African Black Oystercatchers

Urban: Urban habitat shows enormous variation, ranging from woodland areas in older suburbs, through open shrubs in newly established gardens, to the concrete jungle of city centres. Many birds have adapted successfully to these habitats and live alongside humans, common examples being the Hadeda Ibis and Cape Wagtail, both seen frequently in our gardens.

Cape Wagtail having a dip in a bird bath

Greater Double-collared Sunbird